To: Timothy

From Janet & Ge

Before The World Grew Old

North American Indian
Legends and Folk Tales

Also by Mavis Micklethwaite

A WALL FOR THE CUCKOO
THE RED DRAGON
THE ENCHANTED BIRDS
THE MIRACULOUS COW

Before The World Grew Old

North American Indian Legends and Folk Tales

re-told by

Mavis Micklethwaite

Illustrated by Anne Mieke

MACDONALD AND JANE'S · LONDON

For Richard and Charles

ISBN 0 354 08054 7

First published in Great Britain in 1978 by
Macdonald and Jane's Publishers Limited
Paulton House
8 Shepherdess Walk
London N1 7LW

Printed and bound in Great Britain by
Billing & Sons Limited
Guildford

CONTENTS

1. Grandmother Spider captures the Sun. *(Cherokee)* — 1

2. The Bear Star. *(Musquakie)* — 7

3. How Hare brought fire to his Grandmother. *(Menominee)* — 12

4. Coyote and the Locust. *(Zuni)* — 18

5. The Boy who travelled westwards. *(Iroquois)* — 25

6. Why the Bear waddles. *(Comanche)* — 32

7. The Huntress and the Cannibal Demon *(Zuni)* — 38

8. The Helpful Rabbit. *(Passamaquoddy)* — 47

9. Lox and the Wolf Chief. *(Passamaquoddy)* — 53

10. The Gopher and the Runners. *(Zuni)* — 58

11. The Winter Hunt. *(Pawnee)* — 64

12. Partridge and the Sheldrake Duck. *(Passamaquoddy)* — 71

13. The Thunder-stone and the Lightning-shaft. *(Zuni)* — 78

1

Grandmother Spider catches the Sun

At the beginning of time, before the sun came to the world, it was dark everywhere. No one could see anything, and the animal people kept bumping into one another and falling over rocks and into rivers, and scratching themselves on thorny bushes.

'I wish we had some light,' one of them would say. 'Then we could see what we were doing.'

And another would say, 'Yes, we could do with some light. I wonder what has happened to it? There must be light somewhere in the world.'

After a long time the animals grew tired of never being able to find their way about, so they called a meeting to discuss the matter.

The red-headed Woodpecker was the first to speak.

'Listen to me,' he said. 'I have been told that there are some people living far away from here, on the other side of the world, who have this thing called light. This light eats up the darkness so that they can all see one another easily.'

'Is that so?' said the Wolf. 'Then I should like to know why we haven't any?'

'Perhaps if we go to this place and ask the people who live there about it, they will give us some,' the Woodpecker answered.

'Oh yes, they will surely do that,' the other animals cried, and they laughed and stamped their feet as if they were about to break into a dance. All except the Fox, and he remained silent.

'What makes you think they will give us any light?' he asked, when the noise had died down a little. 'They must be very selfish people to have kept it to themselves so long. It would be far better if one of us went to this distant place and stole a piece of it without any of them knowing.'

'Much better,' agreed the Bear. 'I will go. I am big and strong. I can bring back as much as you want.'

'The trouble with you,' said the Snake, 'is that you are far too big and far too strong. The people will hear you trampling through the undergrowth. You will never be able to steal any light without being noticed, and it is sure to be well guarded.'

'If it's not the Bear, then who shall it be?' the other animals asked.

'Let me try,' begged the 'Possum. 'Although you cannot see it I have a fine, bushy tail. I can easily creep up on these people and take a piece of their light and hide it in my fur.'

'That's the answer,' cried the other animals. 'You shall go.'

So the 'Possum got ready for his long journey and set off in the direction of the east, towards the other side of the world. As he scurried along in the darkness, it began to grow lighter. At first the light was very faint, all grey and misty, but as he travelled further the grey became white, like the white of a glistening shell, then whiter still, like ice, and the 'Possum had to screw up his eyes so that he could see where he was going. But he would not stop, even though his eyes hurt as if they were on fire. He went on until he reached the other side of the world and looking up in the dazzling light of the east, he saw the sun.

'So that's where it all comes from,' he said to himself. 'What a size that thing is.'

The 'Possum made himself as small as possible, then he crept up to the sun and broke off a tiny piece. The sun people never noticed, for they were all gazing at the sky.

The 'Possum hid the piece of sun in his bushy tail and set off for his own country, running back towards the west as hard as he could. But the 'Possum did not understand about the sun, as he had never seen it before. The sun was very hot and the piece that he had in his tail burned him badly.

'Oh-oh,' cried the 'Possum, as he scurried towards the west. 'Why did I offer to fetch light for the other animals?' But he kept on running, with his tail held high, for he did not want the other animals to think he was afraid.

'Here I am,' he called, when he reached the animal people. 'I've stolen the light for you.' But when he turned to look behind him he found that the piece of sun had burned his fur right away and left his tail quite bare, and that is how it has always been to this day.

'What use is that to us?' cried the other animals. 'The light has burned up the 'Possum's tail and gone out, so we still cannot see. Now what shall we do?'

'Let me try,' said the Buzzard. 'I have more sense than the 'Possum. I shan't put the light on my tail. I shall carry it on my head.'

So the Buzzard stretched his wings and, soaring into the darkness, set off for the east. As he travelled it grew lighter and lighter and he was able to see further and further. When he reached the other side of the world, he saw the place where the sun was kept. But he also saw that the people who guarded it were watching out for thieves, for they had discovered that a piece had been stolen by the 'Possum.

'They shan't see me. I'm too clever for them,' thought the Buzzard, and although he was already flying very high, he flew higher still until he was no more than a tiny speck above the sun. Then he dived down, as swift as an arrow in flight, and snatched a piece of it in his claws.

'That was easy,' he said to himself, and placing the piece of sun on his head, he flew back across the world. But he discovered, just as the 'Possum before him had discovered, that the sun was very hot and it burned his head, just as it had burned the 'Possum's tail.

'Oh,' cried the Buzzard. 'How my head is being scorched.' But he would not throw the piece of sun away in case the other animals might think he was afraid. When he reached them, no one was any better off, for the light had gone out. But the sun had burned all the feathers off the top of his head and left him bald, and that is how the buzzard looks to this day.

'You are no wiser than the 'Possum,' said the Fox. 'It is still as dark as ever here.'

'What are we to do,' shouted the other animals. 'We shall never see one another.'

'Oh yes, you shall see,' said a very small voice. It was so small it seemed no more than a whisper, but all the animals heard it. They stopped arguing and looked about them in the darkness.

'I can help you,' said the voice. 'I can think of a way to capture the light.'

'Who are you?' asked the Fox. 'You must be very small, for your voice is hardly as loud as the rustling of a leaf.'

'I am Grandmother Spider,' said the tiny voice. 'I am so small no one would ever see me if I went in search of the light. I will go to the other side of the world for you and steal some.'

'Very well,' agreed the other animals. 'You shall go this time.'

Grandmother Spider scuttled to and fro in the darkness, searching and searching until she found a small piece of damp clay.

'That is what I want,' she whispered to herself, and scooping it up with her feet, she made the clay into a little, round bowl. Then she set off towards the east, towards the light, running as hard as she could with her bowl, and spinning a thread behind her so that she would know which way to return.

When she reached the other side of the world, it was just as she had thought. The sun people never noticed Grandmother Spider scuttling along the ground because she was so small. Some of them were gazing at the sky to see if the Buzzard would return, and others were looking towards the darkness to see if the 'Possum was on his way back.

'What a thing it is to be such a small creature,' thought Grandmother Spider, and she crept up to the sun and broke off a tiny piece and placed it in her bowl. Then she turned and ran back along the thread she had spun, while the little piece of sun burned away in her tiny dish.

'Here comes the light at last,' the animal people shouted, as Grandmother Spider approached, spinning her way back along her thread. 'How golden it is! Now all the sky is bright. We can see everything. We can see the whole world.'

'Can you see this as well?' asked Grandmother Spider, and she showed them the little bowl that she had made from a tiny piece of damp clay and which the sun had baked as hard as a rock while she was carrying it back to the other animals.

'How useful that will be,' exclaimed the animals. 'Perhaps we can do the same thing for ourselves.'

And that was how bowls came to be made. First they were scooped out of damp clay and left to dry in the dark, just as Grandmother Spider's little bowl had dried as she scuttled through the darkness to steal the light. Then they were put out in the sun to bake until they became as hard as rocks. This was the second thing Grandmother Spider did for the animal people long ago, when she captured the sun for the world.

2

The Bear Star

It was winter, but a long time ago. The snow came, falling from the sky, whirling in the wind, covering the ground, making the world a quiet place, but very cold.

There were three young men living at that time who were hunters. One morning, before sunrise, the three hunters left their village and followed a trail that led far off into the snowy wilderness. The oldest hunter took his little dog, Hold Tight, with him.

They walked for a long time, first by a frozen river and then through a wood and the only sound to be heard was the noise they made as they brushed through the snow, and the scuffling of Hold Tight as he ran first one way and then another. There were no other animals to be seen anywhere.

Presently they came to a small, tree-clad hill and the oldest hunter stopped to search the trail that twisted and climbed the slope in front of them. Hold Tight sat on the path and waited, for he always liked to copy his master.

'Look,' said the oldest hunter at last, 'I can see some tracks. We are lucky to find any at all in this freezing weather. We had better follow them and see where they lead.'

The three hunters followed the tracks up the hill with Hold Tight trotting obediently behind them. They had not gone far before they came to a cave.

'I'm sure a bear lives there,' the oldest hunter said, gazing at the dark opening on the hillside. 'It has the smell of bear about it and the tracks in the snow are those of a bear.'

'Then we must drive it out and kill it,' said the second hunter. 'There are no other animals around here for us to hunt.'

'Which one of us shall go into the cave?' asked the youngest hunter.

'I will,' the oldest hunter replied and picking up a stout stick, he crawled in at the opening. When he got used to the darkness, he saw that a huge bear was lying asleep on the ground, so he raised his stick and struck it across the nose. The bear woke with an angry roar and sitting up, stared savagely at the hunter. Seeing how fierce he was, the oldest hunter turned and ran out of the cave and throwing his stick away, seized his bow instead.

'Look out,' he shouted to the other two hunters. 'The bear will soon come charging out. When he does we must try to kill him.'

But the bear was too quick for them. Crashing past them out onto the hillside, grunting and roaring as he went, he set off through the snow.

'Stop him,' shouted the oldest hunter. 'What a size he is.'

'Look,' cried the youngest hunter, 'he's going towards the Land of Cold Weather. He's running towards the north. We mustn't let him reach there. We shall freeze to death if we have to follow him as far as that.'

The youngest hunter set off towards the north, running as if the wind were at his heels.

'Go back,' he shouted to the bear as soon as he was near enough. 'The north country is too cold for you. You will freeze to death there.'

The bear was so frightened he turned and ran off another way.

'Look out,' shouted the second hunter. 'He's going towards the land where the sun comes from. He's going towards the east. It will be too bright for us to follow him there,' and the second hunter set off, running as if he were a whirlwind, racing eastwards. He caught up with the bear and drove him back.

But the bear was still frightened and ran off again.

'Hurry,' shouted the oldest hunter. 'We must catch him this time. He's going to the far-off country, where the sun falls below the world at the end of the day. He's going towards the west.'

The three hunters and Hold Tight, the little dog, now ran after the bear as if the lightning were chasing them. They ran so fast they thought they must be floating above the ground. But the bear still kept ahead of them. Presently the oldest hunter stopped running and looked down. He saw the snow glittering far below him, and the trees poking up amongst the hills and valleys like little sticks.

'Stop,' he shouted to the other two hunters. 'We mustn't chase the bear any further. He's leading us up into the sky. Look, Grandmother Earth is already a long way below our feet.'

'We must go back before it's too late,' cried the youngest hunter.

The hunters turned and tried to run back towards Grandmother Earth but they found they could not do so. The bear had led them too far up into the sky, away from the world.

'Perhaps if we kill the bear we shall be able to return,' said the oldest hunter. 'He must have cast a spell over us.'

So the three hunters and Hold Tight set off after the fleeing bear once more and this time they ran fast enough. They not only caught up with him but killed him and cut off his head.

'Help me lift the bear's head,' said the oldest hunter. 'We'll throw it away out there towards the east.' He was so angry to have been led up into the sky that he wanted his revenge. That, he thought, would be the end of the bear, but he was wrong. For then and ever afterwards, when dawn broke in the east on a winter's morning, a group of stars in the shape of a bear's head could be seen low down in the sky. And as they shone then, so they still do to this day.

But the hunters in the sky were still angry with the bear for leading them away from the earth, so next they cut his backbone away and threw it towards the north. Yet, still, that was not the end of the bear, for ever afterwards, when the coldest time of winter came to the world, a group of stars in the shape of the bear's backbone shone in the northern part of the sky.

'Now we'll go back,' said the hunters. But no one ever saw them again, for the sky kept them to herself, and they too became stars.

That is how some of the stars came into being. When darkness comes to the world, the four stars that became the bear star, glitter like tiny pieces of ice. Behind the bear are three big stars, shining like star-moons, and those are the three hunters, for ever caught in the sky. But there is still one more star, a very small star, hardly as big as a drop of frozen water. That is Hold Tight, the little dog, still running obediently after the three hunters.

3

How Hare brought fire to his Grandmother

Once, in the first days of the Indians, Nanabushu, the Great Hare god, lived with his grandmother. Sometimes he went about in the form of a man and sometimes in the form of a hare, whichever he found most useful at the time.

One day, when he was living in the form of a man, he said to his grandmother, 'Are there any people besides us living in the world?'

'There are some,' answered his grandmother, 'but a long way from here. You must cross the sea to find them.'

'That ought not to be difficult,' Hare said. 'Tell me, grandmother, do these people have the thing that is called fire burning in their house to keep them warm when the weather grows cold?'

'Yes, they have that,' his grandmother replied.

'Then I must go and find it and bring some of it here,' said Hare. 'We can keep it by for winter.'

But his grandmother did not like this idea at all. 'You must never try to do that, grandson,' she said. 'The fire is too well guarded. An old man sits beside it all day making nets, and although he has two daughters who go out into the world, he never leaves the house. He will kill you if you go there.'

'No he will not,' said Hare. 'I shall be far too cunning to let that happen,' and he said goodbye to his grandmother and set off in search of the old man's home.

Hare followed the path that led from his grandmother's house until he reached the sea and then he saw just how far it stretched into the distance. He could barely see the land on the other side. But Hare never minded difficulties, large or small, because he always knew how to deal with them.

'I wish the sea would freeze until it was as thick as the bark of a birch tree.' he said, then he sat down and waited for that to happen. And it did happen just as he asked. The waves stopped falling on the shore and the water became covered with a layer of ice as thick as the bark of a birch tree.

'Now I shall become a hare instead of a man,' said Hare, and that happened also, just as he wished. As soon as he had become an animal, Hare scampered onto the ice and ran across the frozen sea, slipping and slithering as he went. But he forgot to freeze the waves that fell on the far shore, so when he reached them they picked him up and tossed him onto some rocks as if he had been a piece of driftwood.

Hare sat up and shivered and looked about him. He saw that the waves had thrown him up near a stream of fresh water that flowed across the shore to the sea.

'I am colder now than I have ever been,' he thought, 'and wetter. I wish one of the two daughters would come to the stream to fetch water for her old father. I am sure that if she saw me in this state she would take pity on me and carry me back to her house.

Hare lay down again. Presently he heard the sound of footsteps coming along the path that led to the stream and, opening his eyes, he saw a woman, the younger of the two daughters, walking towards him.

'Oh, you poor creature,' cried the woman, as soon as she caught sight of Hare. 'I have never in my life seen anything quite so wet and bedraggled. You must have fallen in the stream,' and she bent down and brushed some of the water from Hare's fur.

'You can't stay here,' she went on. 'You'll die of cold before morning.'

The woman was very kind to Hare. She took off her robe, wrapped him up in it and carried him home in her arms.

'Sister,' she called, as she entered the house, 'I found this poor creature by the stream. He must have fallen into the water, for his fur is drenched and he is shivering with cold.'

The older sister looked at Hare wrapped up in the robe. 'What do you think you are doing?' she said. 'You know how angry our father gets when anything is brought into the house. He will make you throw the creature out.'

'What harm can a hare do?' the younger woman

asked. 'Besides, I shall let him go as soon as his fur is dry.'

The younger sister carried Hare to the fire and laid him down beside it. 'The fire will dry his coat nicely,' she said.

Hare stretched himself out beside the flames and looked about him. At once he saw the old man seated in a corner making a net, just as his grandmother had told him.

The two sisters now began to play with Hare, teasing him gently and making him wriggle and jump about by the fire. But the noise they made disturbed their old father and he looked up from his net-making and scolded them.

'How do you expect me to work if you laugh and shout like that?' he cried.

'Look father,' exclaimed the younger sister, 'I found this poor hare by the stream. He must have fallen in, for his coat is all wet. I have laid him by the fire so as to dry his fur. Don't you think he's a nice little thing?'

'Why do you never do what you are told?' shouted the old father. 'Haven't I said often enough that no living creature must enter the house? You have heard about evil spirits. I have warned you and warned you of them. They are as cunning as the night that steals the evening light from us. That animal could easily be one of them.'

'How could such a poor, bedraggled creature be an evil spirit,' laughed the youngest sister. 'Why don't you look for yourself and see how delightful he is?'

'Put him out, I tell you,' answered the father. 'Do you never listen to a word I say?'

'Oh I'll put him out,' replied his daughter, 'as soon as

his fur is dry. I don't mean to keep him here for long,' and she bent over Hare and stroked him lovingly.

'I must be dry by now,' Hare thought. 'I wish a spark from the fire would fall on me.'

The younger sister picked up a piece of wood and threw it on the fire. The wood spluttered and sent sparks flying about the room. One of them fell on Hare and because his fur had now become as dry as an old, discarded bone, it set him alight. Hare leapt to his feet and rushed from the house.

'Just look,' cried the younger sister in alarm, 'the hare is running away with some of our fire.'

'What did I tell you,' shouted the father. 'The hare is an evil spirit in disguise and he came here to steal from us.'

The old man also rushed out of the house and ran to get his canoe, for he saw that Hare was making for the sea. But he soon found that his canoe was no use at all because the sea was frozen from one shore to the other. And there was Hare, scampering away across the ice, shrieking out for his grandmother, his fur burning with the stolen fire.

'It will burn him up and it serves him right,' the old man shouted angrily as he watched Hare disappear into the distance. 'The silly creature knows nothing of fire.'

But the fire did not burn Hare, for he kept on running. As soon as he reached home he rushed into the house and called out to his grandmother, 'Grandmother, grandmother, brush the fire from my fur for I am burning away.'

His grandmother seized a stick and brushed the fire from her grandson's coat and the sparks falling on the stick set it alight.

'That's just what I wanted,' said Hare, and he snatched the stick from his grandmother and stuck it into a pile of wood, which caught alight also.

'Well, grandmother,' said Hare, 'now we have all the fire we want. We shall neither of us ever feel cold again.'

But from that day to this, each time summer has come to the world, Hare's descendants have had a burned-up look about their coats, to remind them of how Nanabushu brought fire to his grandmother.

4

Coyote and the Locust

Once, on one side of a cliff strewn with rocks, there lived an old Coyote, and on the other side, near to a pine tree that had lost its needles, there lived an old Locust.

One day, when the sun was shining, Coyote left his wife and family at home and went out hunting. About the same time the old Locust also saw that the sun was shining, and crawling out of his home he made his way to the pine tree that had no needles. He climbed up the tree and hooked himself onto a branch.

'This is just the right tree to have close to one's home,' he thought. 'Nothing stops the sun from shining on every twig. I don't care for a place that's too shady.'

The Locust closed his eyes and opened them again. 'I feel restless,' he went on. 'There must be something I can do? Perhaps a little music would be nice.' So the Locust picked up the flute that he usually carried with him and began to play.

'I could sing, too,' said the Locust, putting down his flute. Gazing up at the sky he began to sing, 'I'm a Locust sitting on a pine-tree bough, singing away and playing my flute. How my song dances amongst the rocks.'

'So it does', said Coyote, who happened to be passing the pine tree as the Locust sang his song. 'And what a flute player that old Locust makes,' he added, and pausing on the path he shouted out, 'How well you sing and play, old Locust.'

'Do I really?' said the Locust. 'Well, I try,' and he went on with his song.

'It grows better and better,' said Coyote. 'I wish you would teach me your music. I have a large family of children at home and if I sang your song to them, it might keep them quiet for a while. They're a noisy lot.'

'If you want me to,' the old Locust answered, 'you had better listen,' and he sang his song again to Coyote.

'Let me try, just to see if I've got it right,' Coyote said when he had finished, but his voice was nothing like as fine as the old Locust's, and he forgot half the words.

'That's no good,' said the Locust. 'You must get it right if you mean to teach it to your children. Try again.'

Coyote tried again and this time he managed better. 'There you are,' said the old Locust. 'You only need to think carefully, then you'll remember it. Goodbye.'

'Goodbye, old Locust,' answered Coyote and he

turned and loped back along the path towards his home. As he went along he sang the Locust's song to himself so that he would not forget it, for Coyote had never possessed a particularly good memory. While he was singing he kept his eyes fixed on the sky, since he found it less distracting than looking at the path in front of him.

Now there was an old Gopher who lived in a hole not far from the Locust's pine tree. He heard the racket that Coyote was making with his song, and saw him loping along the path with his head in the air.

'What a terrible noise Coyote's making,' he said crossly. 'He's spoiling the day. Why can't he be quiet?' The old Gopher scratched around in the earth, but the sound of Coyote's singing still reached him underground.

'I shall have to put a stop to that,' he said to himself and scurrying up to the surface once more he set to work to make the hole twice the size. Then he sat down and waited.

'How my song dances amongst the rocks,' sang Coyote, and tumbled head over heels into the hole. The fall quite knocked the wind out of him and he lay there gasping and panting. Then he rolled over and some sand trickled into his eyes.

'What did you want to do that for, you grubby-coated old Gopher?' Coyote shouted angrily as he sat up and blinked. 'You don't usually dig such a large hole as this.'

'No,' said the Gopher. 'I wanted to stop you singing.'

'Well, you won't do it that way,' Coyote snapped, and he leapt out of the hole. But when he tried to remember the words of the song, he found that he had entirely forgotten them.

'You idiot, Gopher,' he shouted. 'You've given me such a fright I can't even remember the tune. I'll have to go back to the Locust and get him to sing it to me again. You've quite spoiled my day,' and he turned and ran back to the pine tree.

The Locust was still sitting hooked to his branch, singing and playing his flute.

'Ah, I'm glad you're still here,' Coyote said. 'That silly fool of a Gopher dug a hole for me and I fell into it. It gave me such a fright it quite put the song out of my head. Will you sing it for me again?'

The Locust was not at all pleased to see Coyote sitting below him on the path again, but he knew the only way to get rid of him was to do as he asked.

'I'll sing it for you just once more,' he answered, 'and make sure you don't fall into any more holes.'

'I shan't,' said Coyote. 'Once is enough,' and he listened with great attention as the Locust sang his song.

'Oh, I remember it now,' Coyote said, when the old Locust had finished. 'I'll hurry home before I forget it,' and he set off at a fast trot back towards the rocky cliff.

'My children will be very pleased when they hear this song,' he said to himself as he ran along the track. 'I'd better sing it again just to make sure I don't forget it. "How my song dances – ".'

But at that moment there came such a fearful noise in front of him that Coyote pulled up with a jerk. A flock of pigeons flew up from the shelter of some bushes.

'What a noise you're making,' they cried, beating their wings and scolding him angrily. 'Go away and leave us in peace.'

Coyote sat down, shaking and panting. It was the second fright he had had that morning.

'You great feathered fools,' he shouted. 'Why shouldn't I make a noise if I want to? Besides, it wasn't a noise. I was singing.'

'You may call it that, I'm afraid we don't,' said the pigeons, and they squawked and fluttered their wings and flew away in disgust towards the cliff.

'They're worse than the grubby-coated old Gopher,' Coyote thought angrily, and he tried to remember his song. But of course he had forgotten it again.

The old Locust, who was wiser than he looked, guessed that this might happen, and he also guessed that Coyote would come back and ask him to sing his song once more. Now the old Locust did not like Coyote very much, so he decided that this time he would play a trick.

'It will serve him right,' he thought, and he played the trick that many others of his tribe played from time to time. He blew himself up to twice his normal size so that he split open at the back. Then he climbed out of his skin and leaving it hanging on the branch, he crawled down the tree in search of a stone. He found a nice, light-coloured one, just the right size.

'That will do,' the Locust said to himself, and he crawled back up to the branch to stuff the stone in the discarded skin. 'That's very good,' he said when he had finished. 'It looks just like me,' and feeling very pleased with his trick, he stretched his wings and flew away to another tree.

The Locust had no sooner settled himself on a branch than Coyote came running along the path.

Seeing the old Locust's discarded skin still hooked to the bare pine tree he called out, 'I'm glad to see you're still here. I need some help again. As I was walking along the path, minding my own business and singing my song, some fools of pigeons flew at me and startled every thought out of my head. My song went with them. Will you sing it to me again?'

Of course, there was no answer.

'What's the matter?' cried Coyote. 'Didn't you hear me? I've lost my song again. I want you to sing it to me.'

Still there was no reply.

'Are you deaf? I asked you to sing your song. Look here, old Locust. Do you see my teeth?' and Coyote showed them to him, two fine sharp rows. 'I'll ask you four times to sing your song and then if you don't, I'll snap you up with them.'

The Coyote asked the Locust four times to sing his song, and all he got out of that was silence.

'I'll teach you to ignore me,' yelled Coyote, and he made a leap at the branch and seized the Locust in his jaws. He drove his sharp teeth hard into the skin but instead of snapping the Locust in half as he had thought, he crushed all the teeth in the middle of his jaw against the stone. The force that Coyote used made it even worse, for it drove some of his teeth far down into his gums so that only the tips showed, while others were pushed aside so that now they looked like fangs.

Coyote dropped the stuffed Locust skin and rolled over on his back.

'Oh, my teeth, my teeth,' he roared. 'Oh, how they hurt,' and he rolled from side to side, howling with pain. But that did not help matters at all, so he jumped to his feet and ran off in search of a stream where he could cool his aching mouth. He sat there for a long time, and he never again asked the old Locust to teach him his song.

And that is why, to this day, Coyote's descendants all look as if their teeth have been broken and pushed crookedly about in their jaws. And it is also the reason why, when the Locust comes out to sing his song on a sunny morning, he will often split his skin open and climb out of it and leave it hanging on a tree. By doing that and crawling away to find another place in which to sit, he knows he will be left in peace.

5

The Boy who travelled westwards

Far away, in a wild and lonely place, an old grandmother once lived with her grandson. From time to time this old grandmother would talk to her grandson, giving him good advice.

'When you grow up and go out into the world,' she would say, 'never travel towards the west. If you go that way, harm will come to you. You must always travel towards the east, towards the sunrise.'

'But what can harm me, grandmother?' the boy would ask. 'We live all alone in the world.'

'That is not so, my grandson,' the old woman would say, but she would never tell him any more than that.

The years passed and the boy grew into a handsome youth. Again he went and spoke to his grandmother.

'Grandmother,' he said, 'I'm ready to go out into the world now. But first you must tell me why it is I can never travel towards the west.'

'I will tell you anything else, but never that,' answered his grandmother. But the youth insisted.

'Grandmother, I *mean to* be told.'

'If you must, you must,' she said at length. 'There is an evil being, a fearful monster, who lives in the west and wishes to harm us. If he once sets eyes on you, he will kill us both.'

'That doesn't frighten me at all,' the youth answered. 'I think I shall go and look for him,' and leaving his old grandmother, the youth set out and travelled towards the west.

As evening fell he came to a lake where he thought he would rest for a while. But as he seated himself on the bank, he heard a voice calling to him.

'You there, I can see you even though it's evening and the shadows are long.'

The youth looked about him, across the lake, up at the sky and towards the forest, but he could see no one anywhere. 'You can look as long as you like,' he answered. 'I was thinking of catching some fish.'

'Were you indeed?' roared the voice. 'I'll put a stop to that. I'll send a hurricane and smash your grandmother's house to pieces, so that it litters the ground like firewood. You won't enjoy that,will you? Go home, you stupid fellow.'

'Oh, I don't know,' answered the youth. 'We need some more firewood. It would save me chopping down a tree,' and he left the lake and returned home. But as he approached his grandmother's house, a huge wind sprang up around him. The wind bent the trees as if they were wands, and tore the green summer leaves from their branches and sent them whirling through the air.

'What have you done?' cried the old grandmother, peering from the doorway of her house as her grandson approached. 'You have travelled westwards instead of towards the east and the evil being has seen you. Now we shall both be killed.'

'No we shan't, grandmother,' the youth answered, and he went into the house and closed the door. 'You know very well that I have some knowledge of magic. Now is the time to use it,' and he turned his grandmother's house into a rocky fortress, so that though the hurricance roared and raged about them, no harm came to his old grandmother or himself.

As soon as the storm had passed, the house resumed its normal shape and the youth and his grandmother opened the door and went outside. They found the ground littered with firewood, just as the evil being had promised it would be. But the firewood came from fallen trees, while the grandmother's house remained untouched.

'Didn't I tell you we would be safe?' asked the youth. 'Now we have enough firewood to last us through the winter.'

The following day, the grandson once more left the house, even though his old grandmother begged him to stay at home, and set off towards the west. When he came to the lake he sat on the bank and gazed at the water.

'You there, you're still alive I see,' cried the voice. 'Well, I haven't finished with you yet. This time I'll send a hailstorm to crush your grandmother's house.

You'll like that even less than the hurricane. You'd better go home, you stupid fellow.'

'Oh, I think I shall enjoy a hailstorm,' answered the youth. 'I need some new sharp spear-heads,' and he got up and went home.

As he neared his grandmother's house the sky grew dark, as if night was already falling, and there came a loud, roaring noise from far above him. As he reached the door of the house, hailstones the size of spear-heads began to crash on the ground.

'We shall be killed this time,' cried the old grandmother. 'If only you had stayed at home.'

'Why do you worry so much, grandmother?' said the youth. 'It's quite easy, I shall use my magic again,' and once more he turned the house into a fortress of rock and the hailstones bounced off it harmlessly.

When the storm had passed, the house resumed its normal shape and the youth and his grandmother opened the door and went outside.

'Just as I thought,' exclaimed the youth, gazing about him. 'The storm has littered the ground with spear-heads. I need those for fishing. I'll get some poles to fix them to.'

He went away to look for the poles, but when he returned a while later, he saw that all the spear-heads had vanished.

'Where have they gone, grandmother?' he asked. 'Has someone stolen them?'

'No one has stolen them, my grandson,' answered the old grandmother. 'They went of their own accord. They were not real spear-heads. They were only made of ice. They melted away in the sun.'

'What a cheat,' cried the youth. 'What a trick to play

on anyone. Now watch what I do to the monster.'

'Leave him alone,' begged the old grandmother. 'He will kill you first.'

'He'll never do that,' said the youth, and telling his grandmother to cook a meal for his return, he went out of the house. Then he searched about on the ground until he found a stone the right shape and size and tying a piece of string to it, fastened it round his neck.

'The stone will do for a charm,' he said to his grandmother.

'A stone won't do you much good,' his grandmother answered crossly.

'We shall see,' replied the youth, and following the path through the forest, he travelled westwards again, towards the setting sun.

When he reached the lake, he stood on the bank and looked carefully about him.

'You there, aren't you dead yet?' cried the voice. 'I shall conjure up something so terrible this time that even the other evil spirits who live in the world will be afraid.'

The youth looked in the direction he thought the voice was coming from, and this time he saw a huge head sitting in the middle of the lake, with a hideous face grinning on every side of it. The head looked at him and turned, and looked at him again. Whichever way it turned, a face stared maliciously at the youth, its bulging eyes as black as thunder-clouds.

'So it's you, is it?' said the youth, not at all afraid. 'You wouldn't like it very much if the lake dried up, would you?'

'You can't frighten me,' cried the head. 'The lake will never dry up.'

'We shall see,' answered the youth. He untied the stone from his neck and swung it round above his head. Then he threw it high into the air. The stone rose like a bird above the trees and spun in a half circle from east to west. Then it fell. As it did so, it grew larger and larger. It became first a rock, then a huge boulder, and finally a great mountain peak. When it hit the lake, the water rose in a mighty wave and began to boil, as if it had been heated by a fire.

'You there,' cried the youth. 'How did you like that little blow from my stone? Now where will you find water to drink?' and he returned home and told his grandmother what he had done.

'Plenty of people have tried to kill that monster,' she scolded, 'and no one has succeeded yet. Why don't you leave him alone?'

'I will soon, grandmother,' the youth answered.

The following morning early he left his grandmother's house and went westwards to the lake. When he reached it he saw that all the water had drained away and left the bottom cracked and dry. Its fish lay scattered about, dead, and the only living creature to be seen was a large, green frog, bloated and ugly to look at.

'I know who you are,' said the youth, and he went away into the forest to look for a stick. When he had found a thin, strong one he went back to the lake and crept up on the frog. He dealt it such a blow with his stick that he cracked its skull and killed it outright. Then he returned once more to his grandmother.

'What have you done this time?' the old grandmother scolded again. 'Have you played another trick on that evil monster? Why can't you leave him alone?'

'Oh, I will now,' said the youth. 'He turned into a frog and I killed him with a stick. Aren't you pleased with me now, grandmother?'

After that, the old grandmother was able to live in peace in her house, and her grandson travelled west and east, and no harm came to him whichever way he went.

6

Why the Bear waddles

In the first days of the world, when everything was new, the sun was a difficult being because he always wanted his own way. Sometimes he would climb above the horizon and shine for so long it seemed to the animals there was no such thing as night any more. And that did not please all of them.

'We like it,' the day animals said, 'because we find the darkness a nuisance. We can never see anything.'

'That's all very well, but what about us?' grumbled the Bear, who was a night animal and could see better in the dark. 'We should like it to be night all the time.'

The sun never listened to the animals. He only cared about pleasing himself. But from time to time he grew tired of lodging in the sky and lighting the world, and whenever that happened he would slide back to his comfortable home underneath the earth and sleep for a long time. When he did that, the day animals became angry.

'Now what shall we do?' they asked. 'We can't go on like this.'

But for a long while they did, though the world was a difficult place to live in. At length, however, the animals became so tired of never knowing when it would be light or when it would be dark that they agreed not to quarrel about it with one another any longer. They decided instead to meet and try to find some way of controlling the sun.

'Suppose you all look at it this way,' said Old Man Coyote. 'The sun ought to help the day animals. The night animals can find a dark place somewhere in the world and live there just as easily as they do here. There must be such a place.'

'No there isn't,' said the Bear. 'You know very well that when the sun shines there aren't any dark places left. It would be much better for us night animals if the sun spent all his time asleep underneath the world and never climbed into the sky again.'

'What are you talking about?' cried the Flycatcher. 'Have you all forgotten that the sun is far more powerful than we are? How can any of us tell him what to do? Why, he would never listen.'

The animals looked at one another in silence. No one had thought of that. After a while the Bear said, 'He may be more powerful, but perhaps he will listen to reason if we ask him politely. And to help us decide in as fair a way as possible what would be the best thing for all of us, we could play the game which we animals call the hand-game. If the day animals beat the night animals at it, then they can ask the sun to stay in the sky for as long as they want. But if the night animals win, they can ask the sun to go back under the world and stay asleep.'

'No one could think of a better way than that,' said Old Man Coyote. 'That's what we'll do. Some of you animals had better get the hand-game ready.'

So the Bear, who was quite nimble on his feet then, hurried away to fetch the two small bones, one of which had a mark on it and the other not, and which they used to hide in their hands in turn. The Flycatcher flew away in search of the wands decorated with black crow-feathers. The animals used these to point to the hidden bones and guess which one had the mark on it. And Old Man Coyote went off to find the dogwood sticks which the umpires used to keep the score.

'That's good,' said the Bear, when everything was ready. 'Now we can begin. Owl, you must be umpire for the night animals,' and he sat down comfortably on a log.

'And I'll be umpire for the day animals,' said Old Man Coyote, and he sat down on the grass to keep a close watch on both sides.

'Let me hold the two bones first,' said the Flycatcher. 'Someone on the night side can guess which one has the mark on it.'

The game started and went on for a long time, and sometimes the night animals were in the lead and sometimes the day animals, but either way, nobody won. So they went on playing and, as the time passed, the sun, who was resting in his home underneath the world, began to feel restless.

'I wish they'd hurry up,' he thought. 'I should like to know what the animals want me to do.'

The Bear was also growing tired of the game and his legs were beginning to feel stiff and cramped because he had sat on the log for so long. He kicked off his moccasins so that he could rest his feet.

'That's much better,' he said to himself. 'That's far more comfortable. I can't think why I didn't do that before.'

But the game still went on, and still neither side could beat the other.

'I can't wait any longer,' the sun thought at last. 'I must go and see what's happening.' So he slid out of bed and hurrying from his home, he began to climb the ladder that led up to the sky.

Presently the Owl, who was umpire for the night animals, looked up and saw that the east was growing lighter.

'You'd better hurry,' he called in alarm. 'The game has gone on for so long that the sun's coming from the other side of the world to see who's won.'

'Well, no one has,' said Old Man Coyote, who still sat on the grass watching to see that nobody cheated. 'So we can't tell him. The two sides are exactly equal.'

The sun went on climbing up his ladder, thinking how bored he had been all this time with nothing to do, until at last he reached the top of it and gazed across the world.

'Quick,' cried the Owl. 'Stop the game. The sun is coming. The night animals must go away and hide.'

The Bear was just as afraid of the light as the Owl. 'I had better hide too,' he thought, and jumping up from the log, he looked for his moccasins.

'One, two,' he counted, and bent down to put them on. But he was in such a hurry to catch up with the other night animals, that by mistake he put the right moccasin on the left foot, and the left moccasin on the right foot. Then he ran off.

'That's funny,' he thought, as he stumbled after the fleeing animals. 'I don't seem to be running as well as I might. Perhaps I've been sitting still for too long.'

The moccasins being on the wrong feet made him very awkward, but he went on staggering and waddling away into the distance, as fast as he could to get away from the rising sun.

'Wait for me,' he called to the night animals.

'Then you must run a bit faster,' the Owl called back. 'You're too slow. Can't you see the sun's coming?'

But the Bear could not hurry. He waddled and staggered along as if his feet hurt him, which of course they did, and because he never thought of looking at his moccasins to see if they were on the right feet, he has walked and waddled about in that way ever since.

When the sun reached the top of the sky and was able to see the world more clearly, he asked the day animals which side had won the game.

'No one has,' said Old Man Coyote. 'We haven't finished yet. You came up from underneath the world too soon.'

But the sun told Old Man Coyote that the game had already lasted far too long and that since neither side had won, both must be equal.

'That's quite true,' agreed Old Man Coyote. 'But it doesn't help much.'

'Oh yes it does,' said the sun. 'It helps a lot. Because

you are all equal, I shall help all the animals in the same way. I shall stay in my house underneath the world for half the time, and the other half I shall spend lodged in the sky above you.'

And that was how it happened. From that time on, night and day came in turns, and the animals were able to live comfortably either in the dark or the light, whichever they liked the best.

7

The Huntress and the Cannibal Demon

A poor girl once lived with her aged mother and father at a place not far from a village that was called The Gateway of the Zuni River. There were no young men of the house, as in other families, for the girl's brothers had all died and she refused to marry any of the youths from the village, saying that none of them pleased her enough. Nor would she ask them for help, for she proudly thought she could manage on her own. But although she cooked and washed, and grew beans and corn and pumpkins outside her house, they had no fresh meat because there were no young men to go out hunting for game.

One day, at the beginning of winter, the snow fell, softly at first, but then it grew heavy and the air filled with glittering, white flakes as the wind grew bitter and cold. The poor girl watched the snow cover the plants that she tended outside the house. She knew that unless she found food from somewhere, she and her old mother and father would starve to death.

'But where shall I look?' she said to herself as she saw all the young men of the village set out with their stone-axes and their rabbit-sticks to go hunting. She knew none of them would offer to catch game for her, because she had refused to accept any as a husband.

She returned to the fire and sat down by the side of it to think. But at length she knew what she must do and she went and spoke to her mother and father.

'Tomorrow I shall go out alone on a rabbit hunt,' she said. 'There are no young men in this house who can help us in that way, so I must do everything myself. But the animals will be easy enough to find. I have only to follow their tracks in the snow.'

'You shan't leave this house,' cried the old mother. 'I know what will happen. You will soon get lost and while you are searching for the way home, the wind will freeze you to death.'

'We would sooner remain poor and hungry than have you go out into the world alone to hunt,' the old father added.

But the girl refused to listen to either of them and at last the old man was forced to agree, although he did so unwillingly. 'You must let me help you as much as I can, daughter,' he said and he hobbled away to another room in the house to fetch the stone-axe and the rabbit-sticks that had once belonged to his sons. The old mother also made herself busy with preparations, baking cornmeal cakes in the ashes of the fire.

When they were ready, she strung them on a rope of yucca fibre, as if she was threading beads.

The following morning the girl rose early, long before all the men of the village, and put on a warm dress and deerskin stockings over her moccasins. Then she flung a heavy mantle about her shoulders and fastened the string of corncakes about her neck. The rabbit-sticks that her old father had given her she stuck in her belt, while she carried the stone-axe in her hand. As soon as she was ready, she bade her parents farewell and set off on her journey, through The Gateway of the Zuni River to the wild and lonely country that lay beyond.

The snow covered the winding trail, stretching before her into the distance, glittering and smooth. Presently, when she reached the far side of the valley, she saw some rabbit tracks leading in and out of the rocks and amongst the frozen bushes.

'That's lucky,' the girl reflected delightedly. 'I found those quicker than I thought,' and she began searching for the hollow logs where the rabbits crouched for shelter. Whenever she found one, she split it open with her axe and killed the rabbit with her rabbit-stick. She was so intent on hunting the animals and hanging each dead creature from a rope strung across her shoulders, that she did not notice that the sky had darkened and a snowstorm was approaching.

'My poor old mother and father will be so pleased when they see how many rabbits I have caught,' she said. And although the snow now fell heavily about her, she still hurried on through the shadowy forests of cedar and pine, searching the lonely ravines for more game.

But at last the day began to draw to a close and seeing that she had a good many rabbits hanging from the rope about her shoulders, the girl thought she would return home. However, when she turned to search for the trail that led back to the village, she found that the snow had fallen so deeply that there was no longer any sign of it.

'It must be this way,' she thought, growing a little afraid. But although she hurried on bravely enough, she soon became lost and as darkness fell, knew she could go no further.

'Surely I shan't come to any harm if I shelter amongst the rocks?' she thought. 'I shall find my way home more easily in the morning when it is light.'

She went across to some rocks that she could just see nearby. As she clambered amongst them, she came across a cave with the light of a dying fire still glowing inside it.

'Perhaps some other rabbit-hunters have stopped here before me and left the fire burning,' she thought. 'How lucky I am to find it,' and bending low, she crawled in through the entrance.

The girl soon had the fire burning brightly, for there was a pile of wood lying against the wall of the cave. Then she cut one of the rabbits from her rope and roasted it and ate it with her corncakes. But as she was finishing her meal, she was startled by a long, sad cry, as if someone was weeping out in the darkness because he or she was lost.

'Who can that be?' she wondered, and leaving the warmth of the fire she got up and went to the cave entrance. The lonely cry came again, but this time it seemed nearer.

The girl ran out into the white, glittering snow. 'Here,' she called. 'Oh, do come this way. There is a cave amongst the rocks and I have a fire burning. You can warm yourself by it.'

She waited, calling and calling into the frozen night. Presently she heard, not the same sad, answering cry, but the fearful din of an enormous rattle being shaken close at hand.

'No,' she cried, covering her face with her hands, 'oh, not that. I have been tricked,' and turning, she ran back into the cave and crouched by the fire, shivering and shaking with fright. She knew by the rattle sound that a Cannibal Demon was wandering about, searching for her in the darkness.

'He saw the light of my fire and let out a false cry of distress so that I would answer and my voice would guide him to the cave,' she sobbed. 'Oh, what shall I do now?'

The Cannibal Demon came on towards the rocks, and the girl heard the fallen branches snapping under his huge feet. As soon as he was near enough, the Demon roared out, 'So you're in the cave, are you? I can see your fire burning,' and he shook his monstrous rattle so that it echoed in the darkness as if thunder was rolling about the sky.

The girl shivered with terror and crouched as close as she could to the wall of the cave. 'My poor father and mother,' she whispered. 'They will never see me again.'

Presently the Cannibal Demon reached the cave entrance and shouted, 'I am cold and hungry. Let me in, will you?' He thrust his huge, fearful face with its staring eyes and protruding yellow fangs down at the narrow opening. Then he tried to push his way in, but the entrance was too small for him to squeeze through.

The Demon growled with anger and tried another way to reach the girl. 'Come out, my dear,' he called softly. 'Bring me some food. I won't ask you for anything else.'

'But I have none to give you,' the girl cried, burying her head in her arms. 'I have eaten my meal.'

'Aha, you have, have you,' snarled the Cannibal Demon. 'Surely you must have some rabbits?' and he thrust his horny hands with talons as thick as thigh bones into the cave.

'Yes,' shivered the girl.

'Then bring me some of those.'

But the girl did not dare to move, so she picked up one of her rabbits and threw it at him. The Cannibal Demon swallowed it down at a gulp and cried out for more. The girl threw him another, and then another, until she had no more to give.

'I'm as hungry as before,' roared the Demon. 'Give me more.'

'There are no more,' the girl wept.

'Then throw me your deerskin stockings,' hissed the Demon, and to appease him, even though she knew she did not have long to live, she threw him her stockings. When he had eaten these he called for her moccasins and her belt, then her mantle and her warm dress, until she had nothing left to give him. The Cannibal Demon ate them all.

'I'm still as hungry as ever,' he roared, when he had finished them. 'Let's see what else I can find in the cave,' and seizing his great flint axe, he began splitting the rocks apart at the entrance. The girl listened, frozen with terror, for she knew the Demon meant to force his way in and devour her. The great axe pounded away at the entrance and the rocks shattered and flew apart with each blow, and soon the girl saw the Demon's huge belly, swollen with all the food he had eaten, half-filling the cave in front of her.

Now it happened that in those times, far away in the snow-filled distance, two War-gods lived in their home on the high peak of Thunder Mountain. Although the cave in which the poor girl was trapped was a long way off, they still heard the pounding of the Cannibal Demon's axe against the rocks.

'Of course you know, my brother,' said the elder of the two War-gods, 'that a poor girl has been out hunting in the snow to find food for her mother and father.'

'Yes,' agreed the younger War-god, 'and the girl lost her way and entered a cave where a small fire was burning. That is how the Cannibal Demon found her. In a little while he will have enlarged the cave entrance so much that he will rush in and devour her.'

The two War-gods looked at one another and snatching up their powerful weapons, they flew away into the darkness towards the cave.

'There is the fiend,' cried the elder brother, for he could see just as easily in the dark as in the light. Swooping down eagerly on him, together, the two War-gods reached the Cannibal Demon as he was about to burst into the cave. The Demon let out a roar when he saw the War-gods and swung his axe. But the two brothers were too quick for him. They hit the monster such a blow with their weapons that his head was split open and he fell dead on the ground at their feet.

The two War-gods then entered the cave and called softly to the poor, terrified girl.

'You are safe now,' the elder brother said. 'The Demon is lying dead amongst the rocks.'

The girl lifted her head and looked about her and instead of the terrible, staring face of the Cannibal Demon, she saw two handsome youths, richly dressed.

'I have no clothes,' she said, shivering helplessly. But the two War-gods went out to where the Demon lay, cut him open and drew out her warm dress and mantle, her belt and moccasins and her deerskin stockings. They restored them with their magic, so that they became more beautiful than they had ever been, then they gave them to the grateful girl, who quickly dressed herself.

'What can I do for you in return?' she asked. 'Is there any way in which I can thank you?'

'We will tell you how,' the elder War-god answered. 'It is not right that a woman should set out on a rabbit-hunt alone, nor is it right that a woman should not marry. You must return to your village and accept the first youth who offers himself to you and asks you to become his wife.' They talked to her for a long while and the girl listened and learned many things.

As soon as the sun rose the following morning, the two War-gods left the cave and flinging their weapons among the soapweed plants that grew nearby, they killed a great number of rabbits. Stringing them on a rope, they guided the girl back towards The Gateway of the Zuni River, and very soon she saw smoke rising from the houses in the village.

'Remember all we have told you,' the War-gods said,

and giving her the rabbits, they left her and returned to their home on Thunder Mountain.

When at last the girl reached home, she was welcomed with cries of joy by her old parents, for they had mourned for her throughout the night, thinking that she lay dead in the snow.

'I have learned much while I have been away,' the girl told them as she showed them the rabbits and took off her heavy mantle and her deerskin stockings. 'I have learned that a woman may be a hunter even though she never leaves her own fire. I will marry now, if some youth will have me.'

The girl kept her promise, for one day when a young man who had long admired her came to the house, she willingly accepted him. So from that day, whenever a woman desired to hunt rabbits or any other game in order not to go hungry, she married, and her husband would go out into the world and do her hunting for her.

8

The Helpful Rabbit

In the old times, Great Rabbit was very fat, with no waist at all, and he had a fine, long tail that stretched out far behind him.

One day, when Great Rabbit was sitting on a rock, minding his own business for once, he spied an old man coming towards him. The old man was walking very slowly, looking first one way then another, as if searching for something.

'I'm glad to see you, Master Rabbit,' the old man said when he reached the rock. 'I've been travelling all morning. Walk, walk, walk, that's all I've been doing. Now I'm lost.'

'Are you?' said Rabbit. 'Perhaps I can help. I know all the paths round here.'

'I'm on my way to marry a beautiful girl,' said the old man. 'She's as beautiful as the day's dawning and she has a voice more charming than any bird that sings in the forest.'

'I've heard of her,' said Great Rabbit. 'I know where she lives. I can easily show you the way. Follow me, grandfather,' and he jumped off the rock, and set off running along the path. Presently he stopped and looked back. The old man was hobbling along very slowly, so slowly that even when Rabbit sat down for a while, it took him a long time to catch up.

'Can't you go faster than that?' Rabbit asked. 'We shan't reach the end of our journey by the time the sun sets unless you do.'

'My poor old legs aren't as strong as yours,' the old man replied. 'But I can see you are a very fast runner, Master Rabbit. You'd better go ahead and let me follow at my own pace.'

'Very well,' agreed Great Rabbit and pointing the way along the path, he leapt ahead with a single bound and was soon out of sight.

'My journey's still just as difficult,' the old man thought crossly. 'Master Rabbit isn't much use after all. How can I possibly follow when I can't even see him? I suppose I must try and walk a little faster.'

The old man began to hurry, but this made him stumble, for the path was rough and full of stones, and it was not long before he tripped and fell. Now at that very place there happened to be a deep pit which he could not see, for the hole was covered by a tangled mass of weeds and bushes. The old man tumbled into it headfirst and lay gasping and helpless at the bottom. Presently he sat up and looked about him.

'I can't get out of here,' he thought. 'Where's that Rabbit got to? It's his fault I fell down here.' The old man shouted for help, but Great Rabbit was now so far away that the old man's cries were lost in the forest.

After a while Great Rabbit remembered why he was running along the path and turned to see whether the old man was still in sight.

'Oh dear, I've been too fast again,' he thought, 'but it isn't very easy for me to go slowly. I'd better go back again and look for him.'

The Rabbit ran back along the trail, searching amongst the trees, until he had gone some distance and heard the old man's cries coming from the pit.

'What happened?' asked Great Rabbit, hurrying up to it. 'Well, never mind, grandfather. I'll soon help to get you out. What I need is a stick.' The Rabbit searched about in the forest until he found one he thought might do, then went back and lowered it into the hole.

'I can't reach that,' cried the old man. 'It's only a little stick. It's a long way above my head.'

'Is it?' said Great Rabbit. 'Well, what is longer than that, I wonder?' and he looked at his tail.

'My tail should reach you,' he called out. 'We'll try that.' He sat down by the side of the pit and lowered his tail over the edge.

'Yes, I can reach that,' cried the old man, and he seized hold of it eagerly.

'Wait a moment,' said Great Rabbit. 'I'll give a jump and you start to climb as I do so. Are you ready?' and he leapt into the air. But the old man was heavier than Great Rabbit and gave such a mighty tug on Rabbit's tail that it broke off short, leaving only a small stump behind.

'Oh dear, that doesn't look very nice,' said Great Rabbit, gazing at himself. 'I wonder whether it will grow again? However, you are still in the hole, grandfather, so I must think of another way to get you out. This time you can take hold of me round the middle and I'll try jumping again.'

'Yes, I can manage that,' agreed the old man. He reached up and grasped Great Rabbit round his fat middle and Rabbit gave another leap. But although he pulled the old man out of the pit this time, he was so heavy that Rabbit's back was stretched and almost pulled in two. Rabbit rolled over breathless on the ground.

When he stood up he saw that he had become an entirely different shape. 'Well, grandfather,' he said sadly, 'I'm not the Rabbit I used to be. I've lost my tail and I'm no longer fat round my middle.' Which was very true, for the old man had stretched him out so far and squeezed him in so far, that that is how it has been ever since, all Great Rabbit's descendants having very short tails and narrow waists.

Great Rabbit still meant to help the old man. 'Hurry up, grandfather,' he said. 'We haven't reached the end of our journey yet.'

'Well, don't run so fast this time,' grumbled the old man.

So Great Rabbit went along the path at the old man's pace and although it took them a long time, they at last reached the house where the beautiful girl lived with her parents. The old man was so grateful to Great Rabbit for his help that he invited him to the dance, which in those days formed the marriage ceremony.

The Rabbit was delighted, although when he set eyes on the girl, he wished he could marry her himself.

'Perhaps if I dressed myself up for the occasion she might dance with me a little,' he thought, and he went away to see what ornaments he could find. In the house he discovered some fine ear-rings which he put on his heels for, like all his descendants, he always danced on the tip of his toes. He also found a beautiful bangle, which he hung round his neck. Then he returned to the wedding ceremony.

The bride was waiting for the dance to begin and Great Rabbit, who thought he looked very handsome, took his place opposite her. Now it so happened that the bride that very morning, on crossing a stream near her house, had slipped and fallen in. Although she had dried herself as well as she could, her dress was still damp. But as she started to dance, her skirt began to dry and shrink. It grew shorter and shorter.

'Oh, the poor girl,' thought Rabbit in alarm. 'She'll have no dress at all soon. Then what will she do? I must help her.'

Great Rabbit left the dance and ran back to the house where he found a deerskin. Then he looked for a piece of cord to tie it with, but there was none to be seen.

'Well, I'd better make one,' he thought and cutting a piece of fibre, he began to twist it round and round to make it as thin and strong as possible. He was in such a hurry to make his cord that he put one end between his teeth to hold it firmly. But he pulled too hard and the cord flew out of his mouth and cut his upper lip right up as far as his nose. Great Rabbit called out, for this hurt him, but he still went on twisting the cord.

And that is why, to this day, all Great Rabbit's descendants have hare-lips, as well as short tails and narrow waists.

Great Rabbit returned to the dance and tied the deerskin round the bride to hide her shrinking dress.

'Oh, Great Rabbit,' the girl cried, 'how kind you are. I will dance with you instead of my old husband.'

'You can dance with me as long as you like,' answered the delighted Rabbit, and the girl rewarded him by dancing with him all night, for she was not at all in love with her old husband.

The old man grew very angry as he watched her. 'She is a woman with no heart,' he thought. 'She is not fit to be my wife so I shan't keep her,' and he set off home without saying a word to anyone.

'That's good,' thought the Rabbit. 'I'll ask her to be my wife now.' It seemed to him it would be a nice reward for all the trouble he had taken.

'My first husband was an old man, and now you wish to be my second, Great Rabbit?' the girl said indignantly. 'I don't love either of you,' and she left him and ran away to marry Mikumwess, her own choice, who lived far off, in a beautiful, shadowy forest.

So Great Rabbit was left alone, just as he had been before, and resolved that in future he would try and mind his own business and keep himself to himself. That is why, as everyone knows, rabbits always scamper away as soon as they hear footsteps coming towards them along a path.

9

Lox and the Wolf Chief

In the old days lived Master Lox, the Wolverine. Master Lox caused trouble wherever he went, playing tricks and ignoring advice, but then he was also an Indian Devil and as everyone knows, an Indian Devil always goes his own way. Master Lox fought many battles and was killed just as many times, but he always appeared again sooner or later somewhere, as if he had never been dead at all.

One day, Master Lox found that he was out of luck with the world. It was not treating him as kindly as it should, or so he thought.

It was winter-time, and he was crossing a wide, frozen plain that stretched away into the far distance, so far that he began to think there was no end to it. And a teasing snow fell. It swirled all round him and blew into his eyes, while the wind howled and tore at his fur, so that before long Master Lox began to feel exceedingly miserable and uncomfortable. But he would not give in. The Wolverine was well known for his toughness, and his Indian Devil drove him on. He growled and snarled at the wind and loped over the ground with lowered head, but the distance still seemed as long before him as behind.

Darkness fell, and what little light there was faded from the sky and Master Lox, stubborn as he was, began to wish for some company other than his own. No sooner had he wished it than he heard a long, sad howl across the plain and knew that a pack of wolves was approaching. So Master Lox raised his voice and answered them in their own tongue, for that was another thing the Wolverine could do, he could speak many languages.

The wolves soon reached him and looking at Master Lox they bared their teeth, as is often the custom with wolves. But the Wolf Chief, who was the eldest, treated Master Lox with more respect.

'Perhaps you would like to join our camp tonight, Master Lox,' he said. 'It's not good to be about on your own in this sort of weather.'

'Well, thank you,' said Master Lox. 'I was wondering if I might meet someone with whom I could share my company.'

The wolves collected some sticks and made a fire and sat down by it to warm themselves.

'There's no need to feel shy, Master Lox,' said the Wolf Chief. 'You must come and sit by us and warm yourself as well.'

'I'm not shy,' Master Lox answered, and his Indian Devil caused him to select the best place by the fire. It also made him eat the best of the meat and choose the most comfortable place on the ground to sleep.

When morning came, the Wolf Chief woke Master Lox early and told him of the dangers that lay ahead. 'Listen to me, uncle,' he said. 'It will take you three days to cross this plain. The journey will be a hard one, for there are no places where you can shelter. And you would be unwise to camp at night without a fire, for you will freeze to death. However, I will help you as far as I can. I have with me a spell that will give you three fires, one for each night that you stop. But it will give you no more than that.'

'Is that so?' said Master Lox. 'How do I get this fire?'

'You get it in this way,' answered the Wolf Chief. 'You see this bundle of sticks? You must place them on the ground as if you were about to build a fire, and then jump over them. Then they will catch alight and burn.'

So Lox took the sticks and went on his way, and the plain stretched in front of him and behind him as before. Then the snow fell again, and the wind pierced his fur, so that his thoughts turned to the bundle of sticks the Wolf Chief had given him.

'Is it true or isn't it?' he asked himself. 'I should really rather like to know.' He went on thinking about the sticks, and at the same time growing colder and colder, until at last he said, 'Well, I will try and see if it's true. If it isn't, I've been tricked. If it is, I'll warm myself for a while.'

Master Lox dropped the sticks on the ground and built them into the shape of a fire, then he jumped over them. At once they caught alight and blazed up, just as the Wolf Chief had said, and Master Lox was so pleased that he at once sat down and warmed himself. When he had thawed out, he picked up the sticks and went on his way once more.

But very soon he grew cold again. The tips of his paws began to freeze and his fur became covered with snow, and he lost all feeling in his ears and nose.

'It was far nicer when the world was warm, when summer was here,' he said to himself. 'I felt very happy then.' Master Lox never thought very far in advance for he was not very wise. So he stopped again and built the sticks into a fire and jumped over them, and they blazed up a second time. Then he sat down and warmed himself thoroughly, having quite forgotten that three cold nights must pass before he reached the end of his journey.

'This isn't a bad trick at all,' he thought. 'The Wolf Chief was a clever fellow.'

As soon as he felt better, Master Lox picked up the sticks and went on again. This time he managed to remain on his feet for rather longer, until afternoon came, but by then he was just as frozen as before and his thoughts turned towards a third fire.

'Why shouldn't I stop again?' he asked himself. 'After all, even if the weather is cold now, a thaw could easily set in after an hour or so.' He gazed at the sky. 'Yes, I'm sure it will. The wind will blow the opposite way, the snow will begin to melt, and once it has gone I shan't need a fire.'

Master Lox put the sticks on the ground and jumped over them, and a third fire blazed up. Stretching out beside it he warmed himself.

Afterwards he went on again, and this time he

managed to keep going until darkness fell and it became so cold that the night air froze. Master Lox thought it might be wiser not to go any further until morning, so he stopped and put the sticks on the ground once more and built them into the shape of a fire.

'There's no reason why they shouldn't burn a fourth time,' he remarked, 'or a fifth or sixth either,' and he jumped over them. But of course, nothing happened. So he jumped again. When he had jumped at least thirty times, a little plume of smoke drifted up from the sticks, or so he thought.

'I knew that would happen,' he shouted. 'It's all a question of trying. I shall keep on at it.'

So Master Lox went on jumping, but the little plume of smoke drifted away, and after that there was no more.

'It's a trick after all,' he cried, but he went on jumping, just the same. Then his Indian Devil got hold of him, and he went on jumping and jumping until he became so exhausted that he fell to the ground. And there he lay until he froze to death.

But there are those who say that he recovered, for Master Lox has been seen often enough since, running around and causing more trouble.

10

The Gopher and the Runners

Long ago, some of the people of the world ran a race that was called the Kicked-Stick Race. Not all were good at this race, and some were better than others. But the fastest of all the runners in the Valley of Shíwana were the runners who lived at the Place of the Eagles' Home. No one could beat them.

'Look at us,' they would boast. 'Everyone can see how tall and strong we all are. How can you expect to beat us? You might as well stop trying.'

'Why should we?' the other runners would say. 'The race is open to everyone.'

But no one else ever won, and the runners who lived at the Place of the Eagles' Home grew more and more boastful and proud of themselves until no one could stand their haughty ways any longer. So they called a meeting to discuss how the runners might be beaten.

'We must ask someone else to run the race for us,' one old warrior said, 'and we had better choose the wisest person we know.'

They talked for a long time and thought of a good many people, not all of them as wise as they might have been, but in the end they chose the Gopher. Not a living Indian then could surpass the cunning of that old animal.

'Someone must go and ask him if he will help us,' the old warrior said to the assembled Indians, so a young hunter ran off in search of the Gopher.

The Gopher lived on the side of a hill, near to both the start and the finish of the race-course, for the Kicked-Stick Race began and ended at the same place. The Gopher was busy digging out one of his many cellars when the young hunter came running towards the hill.

'What do you want, my grandson?' the old creature called crossly, none too pleased to see the hunter approach. 'I'm hard at work this morning.'

'I can see that, grandfather,' said the hunter, 'but surely you can stop and listen for a moment,' and he told the old Gopher why he had come. The Gopher was really a kindly old fellow at heart and after listening to the hunter, he said he would leave his digging work that morning.

'I'll run the race for you,' he agreed. 'However, you must tell those conceited runners of the Place of the Eagles' Home that I must run it in my own way and that way, as you all know, is underground.'

The runners of the Place of the Eagles' Home did not mind this arrangement at all. They knew they would still win. But they made one condition.

'Tell your brown-coated old Gopher that from time to time he must put his head above the ground so that we know where he is,' one of them said jeeringly, and the Gopher said he would.

The Gopher waited until darkness fell and then he went to see his brother, who lived nearby at the Place of the Scratching Bushes. This brother was much younger than himself, although he was still very old, and he was so like the first brother that when they were seen together, no one could tell the difference.

'I am to run in a race, younger brother,' said the old Gopher, 'and I've come to ask you to help me. This is how we shall manage it between us. I shall dig two holes at the beginning of the racecourse, which as you know is also the end, one of these holes being a little way from the other. You, at the Place of the Scratching Bushes, must do the same thing. Now I shall be recognised at the start of the race by means of a red plume tied to my head. Younger brother, you must tie a red plume to your head also. Then you must hide in the first hole and as soon as you hear the runners approaching and smell the dust rising as they kick it in the air with their sticks, rush out of your hole as fast as you can and disappear into the second.'

'I will do that for you, older brother,' the younger brother said. 'I shall be glad to see the pride of those haughty runners broken.'

The Old Gopher went next to the Sitting Space of the Red Shell where another brother lived, younger than the first two but so like both of them he could not be told apart either.

'Second younger brother,' said the old Gopher, 'I have come to ask you to take part in the Kicked-Stick Race against the runners of the Place of the Eagles' Home,' and he told the brother what he must do, just as he had told the first younger brother. The second younger brother said he would be glad to help, for he also disliked the boastful runners who had never yet lost the Kicked-Stick Race.

The old Gopher then went to visit five more brothers, each of them younger but still like the others to look at, and each living on a different part of the course.

'I think that should do,' the oldest Gopher said to himself when he had spoken to the last and youngest brother, and he returned home and lay down comfortably in his cellar and went to sleep.

The day set for the race was the fourth day after the old Gopher had set out on his travels in the dark and when the fourth day arrived, there were the runners of the Place of the Eagles' Home, dancing about on their toes to keep themselves as fit and alert as possible. Everyone gathered to watch.

Presently the old Gopher appeared, climbing out of his hole in the ground, a little red plume waving about on top of his head. He took the stick which the other runners had cut for him and placed it on the ground.

'As you know,' he said, 'my feet are so small I could never kick a stick with them, so I shall have to carry it in my mouth instead. However, as I have to dig my way underground and you do not, we shall not be unfairly matched at all.'

'Listen to that old wind-bag dressed up like a

turkey-cock,' one of the runners laughed. 'Carry the stick any way you like. You won't win the race.'

The old Gopher said nothing in answer to this. Instead he dived into the second hole that he had dug a short way from the first, and the race began.

The runners of the Place of the Eagles' Home set off at a fast pace across the plain, kicking up the dust as they went and making a thundering sound with their feet. Presently, some distance in front of them, at the Place of the Scratching Bushes, there was the old Gopher – or so it seemed to them – climbing out of a hole in the ground with his red plume, somewhat dirtier than at the start of the race, waving on top of his head.

'The old Gopher's faster on his feet than we thought,' one of the runners shouted, and he pushed himself forward at an even faster speed. 'But we shall beat him yet.'

On they went, with the dust swirling about them, until they came to the Sitting Space of the Red Shell and there again was the old Gopher, or so the runners thought, climbing out of the hole in front of them. This time the Gopher had stuck some mud on the end of his nose and round his eyes, and even his red plume was heavily streaked with dirt. He looked as if he had been digging hard.

'He wriggles about underground like an old worm,' one of the runners shouted. 'We must go faster than this.'

They did go faster, and the dust cloud grew thicker and the thunder of their feet louder. But then the third Gopher climbed out of a hole in front of them. He had rubbed some water all over his fur and then rolled on the ground, so that he looked as if he had grown hot and dirty with the effort of so much digging. He also pretended that he was tired, for he ran very slowly into his second hole.

'We shall beat him now,' the runners shouted. 'He won't be able to go much further.'

But they were wrong, for the old Gopher, remarkable animal that he seemed to be, stayed the length of the course, although each time he appeared out of a hole in front of the runners, he seemed even more bedraggled and tired than before.

The end of the race, which lay at the same place as the beginning, came in sight at last and as they sped towards it the runners of the Place of the Eagles' Home shouted out words of encouragement to one another. The noise woke the oldest of all the Gophers, who had spent the race sleeping peacefully in his cellar.

'I'd better make haste,' he said to himself, 'or I shan't win after all.' So he rolled about in the dirt, and tore his red plume so that it drooped sadly on top of his head and just as the runners of the Place of the Eagles' Home approached, he crawled out of his hole and dragged himself in an exhausted way to the finish.

After that, it was a long time before those runners ran the Race of the Kicked-Stick again. They returned to their village without saying a word to anyone and they became less scornful of the other Indians who lived in the Valley of Shíwana. The old Gopher also returned to his cellar, as did all his younger brothers, and all of them slept for a very long time. But he woke up one day and told this story to his grandchildren.

11

The Winter Hunt

It was the time of the coming of winter, when the winds blew coldly and bitterly, and ice lay on the lakes, and snow covered the ground.

There was once a boy, a very poor boy, who lived alone with a woman who had lost her husband and had only her young son to keep her company. Because winter had reached them, the woman and her tribe were travelling south in search of buffalo, but although they travelled a great distance, there were no animals to be seen. They climbed the hills to look for them, and searched the white, glistening prairies, but there was no game anywhere for them to kill. They grew weak from lack of food, but they still kept on travelling, looking and hoping, thinking that soon they would be lucky.

The poor boy also became weak and tired with hunger, and one day he could go no further. He sat by the fire, close to the flames, shivering and trying to keep himself warm, but although the others pitied him, they said they could not stay, so they went on and left him alone. The boy was so tired that he lay down and went to sleep.

Presently he woke and was astonished to find that the light had grown stronger and that it was now quite late in the morning.

'I must get up,' he thought, 'or I shall never catch up with my tribe,' but he could not do so because he was too weak, so he lay and looked at the sky. He was not afraid, because he was too tired. Then he noticed that far above him, against the sun, were two strange black dots.

'What can they be?' he wondered. He watched curiously, for they grew larger and larger as they approached. When they drew near enough he saw that they were two swans, beautiful birds, white like the snow around him.

'I must be dreaming,' he thought at first, but then he knew he was not, because the fire still burned beside him. The two swans landed close to the boy and lifted him onto their backs with their wings. The boy wanted to ask where they were taking him, but his weakness prevented him and as the swans rose into the air, he fell asleep.

He woke again, but this time he was lying on the ground in front of a house that was larger than any he had seen before and the air was warm and filled with gentle sounds, as if spring had come. Much to his surprise, the boy found that he also felt a little stronger, so he got up and walked towards the door of the strange house and went inside.

'You are welcome,' a voice said in greeting. 'You will not die now. I am Atius, the great father of many of your tribes.'

The poor boy looked up in astonishment, for he had heard Atius spoken of many times, as had all the members of his tribe. But although they had spoken of him, no one had ever seen Atius, for he lived above them in the skies. The poor boy saw a tall and handsome man with a wise and kindly face. He wore a white buffalo robe about his shoulders, and richly decorated moccasins on his feet. The boy glanced curiously round the room and saw many other chiefs and warriors sitting by the walls, dressed in robes of beaver skin.

Atius spoke to one of the warriors. 'The youth is hungry,' he said. 'He must eat before we tell him of his task.'

'I will find him food,' the warrior answered, and he went away and cut a small piece of meat the size of his finger, and a piece of fat that was no bigger. He gave these to the boy.

The boy was disappointed with his meal. 'That's very little to give me,' he thought. 'I could eat ten times as much as that,' but he began to eat the meat, all the same. He went on eating and eating, while Atius and his warriors smoked their pipes, but he never finished the two pieces of food. When he had eaten as much as he could, he laid the meat and the fat on the ground beside him, and he saw to his astonishment that they were still the same size as when he had started.

'I have been watching your people from my house,' Atius said. 'I have seen how weak and ill they are, and how hunger makes them drag their footsteps. Now I will help you. That is why you have been brought to this place where no other Indian has ever been before.'

'What can I do?' the poor boy asked. 'It's buffalo that my people need, but there are none to be found anywhere.'

'When you return to your winter land, you will find them,' Atius answered, and he gave the poor boy a warm robe to wear about his shoulders, and moccasins for his feet. And because the boy had no weapons, he also gave him a bow and a quiver full of arrows.

'You must use these to hunt the buffalo,' Atius said. 'Now you are ready to return to your tribe.' And he told the warrior who had cut the two pieces of meat to take him back to the swans.

'How am I to find the buffalo?' the poor boy asked. 'No one has told me.'

'You will see as soon as you get back to your world,' the warrior replied, and he lifted the boy onto the backs of the two swans. Then he touched the boy's eyelids and immediately the poor boy fell asleep again.

When he woke a second time he saw that he was lying on the ground once more. Everywhere was still thickly covered with snow and a cruel wind blew about him. Then he saw that the fire had gone out and the ashes grown cold. He jumped to his feet.

'How well I feel,' he cried in amazement. 'I'm stronger than I've ever been before. It must be the strange meat that Atius gave me. Now I must find my people, just as he told me,' and he set off eagerly along the trail.

He travelled fast, running across the snow, so that long before darkness fell, he had overtaken his tribe. He saw with pity in his heart how slowly they were travelling, how they could hardly drag their feet over the frozen ground, and how the children were crying from hunger and weariness.

The poor boy went to the wigwam where the woman lived who looked after him. She stared at him in amazement as he entered.

'Where have you been?' she cried. 'And where did you get that warm, fur robe and those moccasins? Have you been stealing?'

The boy did not answer her. 'Tell me, my poor mother,' he asked, 'what are you doing with that knife?'

'Can't you see?' she replied angrily. 'I'm cutting up my last piece of robe so that I can cook it over the fire. When we have eaten that, there will be nothing left.'

The boy turned and went out into the darkness and shot an arrow into the air, and the woman gazed after him wearily. Then she thought she heard a buffalo snorting.

'I'm ill,' she thought. 'I'm so weak with hunger I thought I heard an animal outside the house.'

The poor boy came back into the house. 'Come and look outside,' he said.

'Look at what?' asked the woman. 'There's nothing out there except cold and ice and snow.'

But the boy persisted. 'Come and see,' he repeated.

So the woman left the piece of robe she was cutting up for food and went outside and there, standing by the door of the lodge, was a large buffalo.

'Where did this come from?' the woman cried. 'How

did you find it? Oh, how thankful I am to see such a large animal.'

But the boy would not tell her where he had found it. Instead he killed the buffalo and the woman wept with relief as she cut enough meat for herself. The rest she gave to her tribe.

The following morning the poor boy said to the woman's son, 'Do you see the hill that lies beyond the camp?'

'Yes,' the son answered.

'Then run to the top of it and tell me what you see on the plain beyond.'

'There won't be anything,' the son replied, but he ran to the top of the hill as the poor boy had told him. He saw nothing anywhere except the snow. He looked in every direction, but the world was white and glittering and still, because it was winter.

He went back to the poor boy. 'It's just as I said. There's nothing to be seen except snow.'

'Yes there is,' said the poor boy. 'Try again. You'll see something this time.'

So the woman's son ran to the top of the hill and looked about him again in every direction, but the prairie was still as empty as before.

'What am I supposed to be looking for?' he wondered. 'The world is dead.' Then he went back to the poor boy and said that he could still see nothing.

'You aren't looking about you as well as you might,' the poor boy answered, and snatching up the bow and quiver that Atius had given him, he ran to the top of the hill himself and shot an arrow into the air. Then he turned and looked southwards, and as far as he could see, the plain was filled with buffalo floundering about in the snow. It was so deep that they could hardly move.

The poor boy went back to the village. 'I have found the buffalo,' he said. 'You can go and kill as many of them as you want. The hunt will be an easy one for once, for the animals are stuck fast in the snow.'

The Indians ran out onto the plain and stared at the herds of buffalo in astonishment.

'None of these were here yesterday,' one said to another. 'How did the poor boy find them?'

But the boy would not tell them, and the Indians killed as many of the buffalo as they needed and returned laden to the village. Now they had enough meat to last them all the winter, and enough skins to make warm clothing for everyone from the oldest to the youngest. They made the boy who had seen Atius and had learned from him how to hunt buffalo in the winter, the chief of their tribe. It was not long before the boy became as rich as he had once been poor, but to the end of his life he ruled his tribe with the wisdom that had been given to him by the great father of the Indians.

12

Partridge and the Sheldrake Duck

Long ago, so they say, Partridge was a fine hunter. He lived far away in a wood that many of the Indians did not know about, although sometimes he came strutting out of it, and then he was seen. But mostly he went the same way along the same trail, carrying his bow and arrows, towards the river.

Partridge had built himself a house in a lonely place under the trees and although no one ever passed his door, he was far from lonely because he had his brother living with him. This brother was so small that he was kept hidden away in a box. And whenever Partridge went out to hunt, which was almost every day, he locked the box and put the key in another place. His brother being the size he was, Partridge was afraid that one of the evil spirits who roamed about the world would creep into the house and seize him, and he would never be seen again.

One day, as Partridge was returning from a hunting trip in his canoe, he saw a beautiful girl sitting alone on a rock by the river bank. She was busy making a moccasin.

'How neatly she sews,' Partridge thought. 'I should very much like to have her for my wife,' so he turned his canoe and paddled softly towards her.

But he was not quiet enough, for the girl heard him coming. She looked up and screamed and threw her moccasin away in a fright. Then she dived into the water and Partridge went home without the wife he wanted, not feeling at all pleased.

The girl swam down to the bottom of the river, where she lived with her mother.

'Where is the moccasin you were making?' her mother asked, seeing her empty hands.

'I threw it away because I was frightened,' the girl answered. 'Partridge, the hunter, was passing in his canoe and saw me. He meant to seize me and take me home to be his wife.'

'If he has seen you, then you must go back,' her mother replied. 'You belong to Partridge now, so you must become his wife, as he wishes.'

The girl was far from happy about this, but she obeyed her mother and went to Partridge's lonely house in the woods. When she reached it, she saw that he was away hunting. The girl was glad of this, for she knew Partridge would like her better if she could find some way of pleasing him before he returned.

'I'll make him a bed of freshly-cut boughs,' she

thought. 'Then I'll light the fire and clean the house.'

She did so, and when night fell, Partridge returned with a beaver he had caught and found her waiting for him.

'Ah,' he said, for he knew what had happened, 'your mother told you to come.'

The girl did not answer, but she watched as Partridge cooked the beaver. When it was ready, he cut the animal in half with a knife. He put one half aside, and the other half they ate between them. In the morning when the girl woke, Partridge had gone and the half of the cooked beaver that had been left was nowhere to be seen.

'Perhaps my husband ate it while I was asleep,' she said to herself.

She busied herself about the house all day and when Partridge returned, he had another beaver with him. This time he gave it to his wife to cook. When she had done so he cut it in half and laid one half aside. The other half they ate between them.

When she woke in the morning, Partridge had gone hunting as before, and the half of the cooked beaver that he had laid aside had also disappeared.

'I wonder what he does with them?' she thought curiously. 'I must find out.'

That night the girl lay down by the fire and pretended to fall asleep at once, but she was careful to close only one eye. Partridge waited for a while and presently, when all was quiet and he thought it was safe, he went and fetched the box in which he kept his little brother. Then he unlocked it and took out a little red dwarf.

'How have you been, brother?' he asked.

'Hungry,' answered the dwarf. 'I see you still have your wife.'

'True,' agreed Partridge, 'but you needn't be afraid of her. She knows nothing at all about you. Here is half a beaver I have cooked for you.'

The little red dwarf took the beaver and ate it quickly, bones and all, for he had a large appetite.

'Now I'll comb your hair and brush your beard for you,' Partridge said, when the dwarf had finished the last scrap.

'Yes, do that,' agreed the little red dwarf. 'They are both in such a tangle.'

As soon as the little red dwarf was clean and tidy again, Partridge put him back in the box and locked him up. Then he hid the key in its hiding-place in another corner of the room.

When Partridge's wife woke in the morning, she saw that her husband had gone hunting again, just as he did every day.

'Well,' she thought, 'why shouldn't I have the dwarf to keep me company for a while? It's lonely in this house with no one to talk to. Besides, how will my husband know if I ask the dwarf not to tell him?'

So she went and found the key and opened the box.

'Won't you come out?' she asked the dwarf. 'Surely you can't like being shut up in the dark all day.'

'Go away,' shrieked the dwarf. 'Lock the box. I like the dark.'

'Please come out for a while,' the girl begged. 'I will comb your hair for you and brush your beard.'

'If you do that, perhaps I might,' the dwarf agreed. 'But you must put me back again as soon as you've finished.'

'Oh yes,' the girl promised eagerly, and she lifted him out and stood him on the ground. But as she touched him she noticed that her hands became stained with red.

'I'll wash that off later,' she thought, and picking up a comb, she began to untangle the dwarf's hair.

'Be careful,' the dwarf said peevishly. 'I don't like having it pulled.'

'I'll be careful,' the girl answered, and she was for a while, but then she forgot and tugged hard at a knot by mistake. The dwarf let out such a shriek at this that the girl dropped the comb in alarm. But as she did so a hideous, grinning monster, one of the evil beings that roam the world, ran into the room and seized the little red dwarf in its bony hands. Then it disappeared into the woods, and Partridge's wife heard the dwarf's shrieks growing fainter and fainter in the distance, like the cry of a wounded bird.

The poor girl was so frightened that she sat down by the fire and sobbed until she could sob no more. 'What shall I do? What shall I do?' she kept crying. Then she looked at her hands and saw how stained with red they had become.

'I must wash that off before my husband gets home,' she thought, so she ran to the river and hastily dipped them in the water. But although she rubbed and rubbed the stain would not go, and more frightened than ever at what her husband might say when he saw them, she went back to the house and sat down to wait.

Towards evening, Partridge returned. When he entered the house she saw that he was empty-handed.

'Were there no beaver in the river?' she asked timidly.

'Maybe there were, but I couldn't find any,' Partridge answered.

The girl tried to think of a way of soothing him, for she could see that he was angry. 'Give me your weapons to put away,' she said, and by mistake she held out her hands. Partridge saw the red stains and at once he flew into a terrible rage.

'I know what you've been up to,' he shouted, waving his arms and stamping his feet. 'You opened the box and took out the little red dwarf.'

'Yes,' sobbed his wife, not knowing what else to say.

'Where is he? Where is my brother?' shouted Partridge.

'A horrible monster came and seized him,' his wife cried. 'Oh, what shall I do?'

'I knew that would happen,' Partridge shrieked. 'I should have locked you up as well,' and he snatched up his bow to beat her. But the girl screamed and ran out of the house towards the river, tripping and stumbling as she went. Partridge ran after her, shouting angry threats and striking the air with his bow.

'I'd rather drown than be his wife,' the terrified girl thought and as soon as she reached the river, she threw herself into the water. 'My life will soon be over now,' she cried.

But, she did not drown, as she had expected. Instead she found herself floating easily on the river, swimming about amongst the water plants and the little eddies that whirled past its banks. She had become a Sheldrake Duck, a beautiful little Sheldrake Duck. Although Partridge saw her when he reached the river and began to search the thickets, he never knew that the little bird bobbing about before him was his wife.

And to this day, the marks of the stain left by the little red dwarf are there on the feet and feathers of the Sheldrake Duck for everyone to see.

13

The Thunder-stone and the Lightning-shaft

Long ago, but some time after the beginning of the world, the two gods of War lived with their grandmother on Thunder Mountain. The War-gods were twin brothers and because in those days they were young, they did much as they pleased. Sometimes they behaved well and sometimes they did not, but now and again something good came out of their wilful ways.

One day, they told their grandmother that they were going out to hunt prairie dogs.

'You are not very good at that,' their grandmother said crossly. 'You play about too much.'

'Oh, but we will be good this time,' they promised, and they went laughing and skipping out onto the prairie, chasing the dogs but not catching any of them.

Presently it began to rain. The rain fell like a waterfall, hissing and roaring all about them. South of the prairie, the thunder rolled and shook the sky, and shafts of lightning zig-zagged this way and that amongst the clouds. Pretty soon the ground became muddy and slippery and the two War-gods could not chase the dogs so well. They flew into a rage and shouted at the storm, for they did not like to have their game spoiled.

'Brother,' said the elder of the two War-gods at last, 'I can think of another game that would be more fun. Suppose we run away to the Land of Everlasting Summer and steal the thunder and the lightning? Then we can play about with the weather ourselves.'

'Our grandmother will not like it if we do,' the younger brother answered. 'You know how cross she always gets. We must not tell her what we are up to. Perhaps we had better catch some prairie dogs after all so that she has something to eat while we are away.'

'Oh yes, we can do that,' agreed the elder brother. 'She will not be nearly so angry when she sees how good we are at hunting.'

But the old grandmother was still not very pleased with them, in spite of all the fresh meat they brought her.

'What are you up to now?' she said next morning, as they dressed themselves to go out again.

'We are going to catch some more prairie dogs for you, grandmother,' they laughed, and skipped away down Thunder Mountain. Then they ran across the prairie to the Land of Everlasting Summer.

The Land of Everlasting Summer was a warm and beautiful place. The mountains glimmered always with the colours of the setting sun, and its valleys held the secret of the sunrise. The two War-gods knew that hidden away in one of those most secret valleys was a red house, the House of the Beloved Rain-gods, who guarded the sacred Thunder-stone and the Lightning-shaft. But when they reached it, the brothers found that it was almost as tall as the mountains that surrounded it, and its red walls were so smooth and slippery they could not climb them.

'We must think of another way to get in,' the younger brother said crossly. 'Let us go and find our grandfather, the Centipede. He will know how to help us.'

So they went away to the place where they knew their old grandfather lived and began lifting one huge stone after another, for it was under stones he spent most of his time, hiding himself away from the sun. In those days the centipede was much larger, so he was quite easy to see. They found him at last, sound asleep, as he always was in the middle of the day.

'Wake up, grandfather,' they shouted, prodding him with their arrows. 'We need your help.'

'Go away,' said their grandfather angrily. 'I don't want to be disturbed just now. Besides the light is far too bright. It hurts my eyes.'

'Please wake up,' the War-gods shouted again. 'There is no one in the world who can help us as well as you can.'

'That is probably so,' agreed the old Centipede, who like many other creatures, never minded a little flattery. 'What is it you want this time? I'll help you if I can, but you mustn't blame me if anything goes wrong. You seem to make a habit of causing mischief.'

'Nothing will go wrong,' said the War-gods. 'All we want you to do is to climb into the red house of the Rain-gods and steal the Thunder-stone and the Lightning-shaft for us.'

'What next? Why don't you go home to your grandmother where you belong?' cried the old Centipede. 'You'll only make more trouble for everyone.'

'Oh, do hurry up, grandfather,' the War-gods said impatiently. 'We only want them for a little while.'

'Well, don't blame me if things turn out badly for you,' grumbled the old Centipede, and stirring his countless legs, one after another, he ran off towards the red house of the Rain-gods. He had no difficulty in climbing those smooth walls, for if one foot slipped, the rest held on. Over the roof he went, and down through the smoke-hole. Then he scuttled across the ceiling to the sacred place where the Rain-gods kept the Thunder-stone and the Lightning-shaft. The gods were sitting with their eyes closed, deep in thought, so they never heard the faint scuffle-scuffle of the old Centipede's feet as he ran across the room. The old grandfather picked up the Thunder-stone in his mouth, even though it was very heavy, and hurried back to the War-gods. He threw it to the eldest brother.

'He has got it,' cried the brother, catching the Thunder-stone as it was about to roll and shake the sky. 'I knew he would.'

'What about the Lightning-shaft, grandfather?' asked the youngest brother. 'I have nothing to play with yet.'

'Can't you wait?' snapped the old grandfather, and grumbling away to himself he went back to steal the blue, shimmering Lightning-shaft in the same way.

'Thank you, grandfather,' cried the younger brother. 'Now you can go back to sleep again,' and seizing the Lightning-shaft he ran back to Thunder Mountain with his elder brother. But they stopped to catch a few prairie dogs on the way, in case their old grandmother should suspect they had been up to no good.

'There you are, grandmother,' they said, when they reached home. 'We told you we were going hunting.'

But the old grandmother saw the tip of the Lightning-shaft gleaming and poking out from the younger War-god's clothes and she knew immediately what it was.

'You've stolen the Lightning-shaft,' she cried, 'and I suppose your brother has the Thunder-stone. Oh, what wicked boys you are. What will you do next? You must take them back at once,' and she seized a stick to beat them with.

'We shall neither of us let you do that,' shouted the War-gods, and they ran out of the room and shut the door and fastened it so that their grandmother couldn't open it. 'Now we can play,' they said gleefully, and they climbed onto the roof of the house. The elder brother rolled the Thunder-stone about. It rumbled and roared and shook the mountain so that it almost split apart. The younger brother sent the Lightning-shaft far out into the sky, where it hissed across the prairie and then returned to him. They played like this for some time, laughing at the racket they were making.

But the noise of the thunder and lightning roaming about the sky soon disturbed the Rain-gods as they sat in their red house in the Land of Everlasting Summer.

'Someone has stolen the worst of the weather from us,' one of them said angrily. 'Who is it?'

'I do not know who stole it, but the two War-gods are playing with the Thunder-stone and the Lightning-shaft on the roof of their grandmother's house,' another replied.

'Then we must punish them,' said the Chief of all the Rain-gods. 'We shall send the wind and the rain as well to Thunder Mountain. They can have all the bad weather there is and neither of them will like that.'

When a mighty wind suddenly arose and tore across the slopes of Thunder Mountain the two War-gods were astonished, and even more astonished when the rain fell so heavily on them that it was like all the rivers of the world rolled into one. But they only laughed and went on with their game.

Soon the rain became so bad that it began to pour in through the roof of the house.

'Stop your game, my stupid grandchildren,' cried the old grandmother. 'You are filling the house with water.'

'What have you got to worry about, grandmother?' laughed the two War-gods. 'You will only get a little wet.'

But the rain water rose and rose and presently it filled the house so that the fire was put out. Still it went on rising, and in a while the old grandmother had to climb up amongst the rafters.

'I shall drown if you don't stop your game,' the old grandmother shouted. 'I wish I could get out there and beat you. The rain has filled the house to the top.'

'Well, swim about, grandmother,' said the War-gods. 'We cannot stop playing just yet. We are enjoying ourselves too much.'

The water went on rising until in the end it filled the house above the rafters and the old grandmother could no longer cry out to her two grandsons. But the two War-gods had to stop their game at last. The Thunder-stone became too heavy to hold and the Lightning-shaft too hot to touch, so the brothers flung them away into the sky. They rumbled and flashed across the prairie to the red house of the Rain-gods, and the Rain-gods caught them and returned them to their sacred place.

Presently the rain clouds parted and drifted away and the twin War-gods sat down on the roof of their house and looked about them.

'What a flood we have caused,' one of them said. 'It is spilling out of the house. I feel hungry. When the water is a bit lower we will climb down and get our grandmother to cook us a meal.'

So they waited, and after a while they were able to slide off the roof on to the ground.

But as they unfastened the door it burst open and the water poured out of the house in a flood, and their old grandmother came tumbling out with it.

'Oh, we have killed our poor old grandmother,' cried the brothers, as they gazed at her in astonishment. 'Oh, and she loved us so much. It was a pity she was always so angry with us. Now she cannot be angry any more. We had better bury her. She would like us to do that.'

So the two War-gods buried their old grandmother by the door of the house and, strange to tell, in four days, a plant they had never seen before grew up from the place. Amongst its shiny leaves there hung long, pointed fruit pods, each as red as the sun when it sets. The two War-gods knew at once what they were.

'Look what our grandmother has given us,' exclaimed the eldest brother. 'She does not want us to go hungry now that she can no longer cook for us. She has sent us the first peppers in the world. They have grown straight out of her cross old heart. Look they are all a fiery red, like the colour of her words when she scolded us.'

'We had better plant the seeds,' said the younger brother. 'One day the Indians will find these peppers and want to grow more for themselves. They will be very grateful to our old grandmother.'

So the two War-gods planted the fiery red peppers all about Thunder Mountain and there the Indians found them. They took the fruit away and planted the seeds and called the place where they did so the Pepper Gardens of Zuni. And their descendants have grown these peppers ever since.

But the two War-gods were still in trouble, for the Rain-gods were angry and wanted to know who had stolen the Thunder-stone and the Lightning-shaft, and the War-gods, as wilful as ever, said it was their old grandfather, the Centipede.

'Then I shall teach him it is wiser not to steal,' replied the Chief of the Rain-gods. 'He may have the Lightning-shaft back, but he will not find it as easy to handle as before.'

Nor was it. The Lightning-shaft was so hot this time that it burned the poor old Centipede and shrivelled him up so that he became very small, and he looked just like a piece of dried skin as he hid himself away under his rock. That is why all the descendants of grandfather Centipede are so tiny to this day, and why they all look as if they have been roasted over a fire.

BIBLIOGRAPHY

Myths and Legends of the North American Indians – Lewis Spence.
The Algonquin Legends of New England – Charles G. Leland.
Zuni Folk Tales – Frank Hamilton Cushing.
American Indian Mythology – Alice Marriott and Carol K. Rachlin.
The Story of the American Indian – Paul Radin.
The Leaping Hare – George Ewart Evans and David Thomson.
Pawnee Hero Stories and Folk Tales – George Bird Grinnell.